29

S0-AGW-344

Keeping Unusual Pets

POTBELLIED PIGS

Tristan Boyer Binns

Heinemann Library
Chicago, Illinois

Designed by Roslyn Broder
Photo research by Amor Montes de Oca
Originated by Dot Gradiations Limited
Printed in China by WKT Company Limited

08 07 06 05
10 9 8 7 6 5 4 3 2

Library of Congress Cataloging-in-Publication Data

Binns, Tristan Boyer, 1968-
  Potbellied pigs / Tristan Boyer Binns.
        p. cm. -- (Keeping unusual pets)
Includes bibliographical references (p.   ).
Contents: What is a potbellied pig? -- Potbellied pig facts -- Babies and piglets --
Is a potbellied pig for you? -- Choosing your potbelliedpig -- Your potbellied pig's home
-- Caring for your potbellied pig --Feeding your potbellied pig -- Training your potbellied pig
-- Visiting the vet -- Some health problems -- Keeping a record.
ISBN 1-4034-0828-9 (HC)
  1. Potbellied pigs as pets--Juvenile literature. [1. Potbellied pigs as pets. 2. Pets.] I. Title. II. Series.
  SF393.P74B56 2004
  636.4'85--dc22
                            2003015539

Acknowledgments
The author and publishers are grateful to the following for permission to reproduce copyright material:
Icons, pp. 5b, 7, 8b, 12, 15, 17, 20, 21, 22t, 23, 24, 25, 26, 27, 28, 31, 23b, 33, 34, 41 Greg Williams/Heinemann Library; pp. 4, 6 William J. Weber/Visuals Unlimited, Inc.; p. 5t Ernie Janes/NHPA; p. 8t E. Henumentah Roo/Photo Researchers, Inc.; pp. 9, 10, 11, 13, 16, 18, 19b, 22b, 29, 35, 36, 39b, 40, 45t Nancy Shepherd; p. 14t Jeff Greenberg/Visuals Unlimited, Inc.; p. 14b Lawrence Lucier/Getty Images; p. 19t Bill Greenblatt/Getty Images; p. 30 Norm Betts/Photographer's Direct; pp. 32t, 38, 39t, 43, 45b Carol Infalt, Pigs Home N Rome; p. 37 Sean Cayton/The Image Works; p. 42 Mary Kate Denny/Photo Edit; p. 44 Heinemann Library

Also, special thanks to expert reader, Nancy Shepherd, Pig O' My Heart Potbellies Farm, Rocheport, MO.

Cover photograph by Tim Davis, Renee Lynn/Photo Researchers, Inc.

Every effort has been made to contact copyright holders of any material reproduced in this book. Any omissions will be rectified in subsequent printings if notice is given to the publisher.

No animals were harmed during the process of taking photographs for this series.

Contents

Some words are shown in bold, **like this.** You can find out what they mean by looking in the glossary.

What Is a Potbellied Pig?

Potbellied pigs are a kind of **miniature** pig. All miniature pigs are related to full-sized farm pigs. All pigs are **mammals.** They are **warm-blooded,** give birth to live babies, and feed their babies with milk.

What is a miniature pig?

Miniature pigs can weigh between 60 to 175 pounds (27 to 79 kg). This may seem big to you, but they are miniature compared to ordinary pigs.

While some people on farms keep full-sized pigs as pets, most pet pigs are miniature pigs. In the United States, the most common pet miniature pig is the potbellied pig. In this book we will talk about potbellied pigs, but most of the information is good for other miniature pigs, too.

Farm pigs can weigh 1,000 pounds(455kg)!

Need to know

Having a potbellied pig is a huge responsibility. You should decide with the rest of your family if you are ready to take it on. Use the information in this book as a starting point, and talk with your veternarian and other local potbellied pig owners before you decide. Most countries have laws protecting animals. It is your responsibility to make sure that your potbellied pig is healthy and well cared for. Always take your pig to the vet if it is ill or injured.

What kind of small?

Miniature pigs are bred to be smaller than ordinary pigs. **Breeders** choose parents with the best features to produce piglets that look and act more like the ideal they are trying to reach. Some miniatures are midgets, and others are dwarfs.

Every part of a midget is the same amount smaller than the same part of a ordinary pig. A dwarf is smaller than an ordinary pig, but parts of it are different amounts smaller. Usually it has shorter legs, but a bigger head and longer body than an ordinary pig's. Potbellied pigs are dwarfs.

Other miniature pigs

Miniature pigs in the United States include:
- Potbellied or Vietnamese Pigs
- Juliani or Painted Miniature Pigs
- Yucatan or Mexican Hairless Pigs
- Guinea Hog
- Ossabaw Island Pigs

Kune pigs are also miniature pigs.

Potbellied pigs make great pets for people who know what to expect.

5

Potbellied Pig Facts

The best way to start learning about potbellied pigs is to see how ordinary pigs live in the wild. Pigs will try to eat almost anything. All pigs eat both plants and animals. Wild pigs spend much of their time searching for food. They use their snouts to **root** through soil, looking for insects and plant roots. They use their incredibly strong sense of smell to find food above ground, such as eggs.

Pigs usually search for food and do all their activity during the day. They rest at night. In the wild, pigs live in many different habitats. They tend to stay in one area, looking for food in the same places during the day and going back to the same resting place at night. They even go to the bathroom in the same few places.

Wild pigs use their snouts to look for food.

Skin

Pigs have thick, bristly skin. Bristles are like strong hair. Pigs shed their bristles about twice a year. Pigs love to soften their skin. Even if a pig has clean, well-oiled skin, it will **wallow** and scratch it to make it feel even better. Pigs love to wallow in mud. They will also wallow in chewed up hay, dry soil, and blankets.

Snouts

Pigs have amazing snouts. They are bendable and strong. Their snouts can dig deep holes as pigs look for food or dig a hollow to cool off in. Pigs get a lot of information by touching things with their snouts, just as people use their fingers. Because pigs root through soil, they can pick up a lot of germs through their snouts. They can get colds and coughs this way.

A pig snout has bones and muscles to make it move as the pig wants. It is a very useful tool.

Life in a herd

Pigs live in herds. A herd has a **pecking order** that ranks each pig. As soon as pigs are born, they start to look for their place in the pecking order. Pigs mostly use their teeth to defend their place in the herd by biting or chasing away challengers. When the pecking order is sorted out, herds are mostly peaceful. In the herd, pigs talk to each other by grunting, squealing, and snorting. They also bump and rub each other to keep in contact.

This herd of wild pigs is looking for food.

A new kind of pet

Eighteen potbellied pigs were brought to Canada in the 1980s. These were probably the first in North America. Potbellied pigs had been bred from normal pigs in Asia to be cute and easygoing. By the 1990s, **breeders** were making sure all the people who wanted pet potbellied pigs could find them!

This looks like an ideal potbellied pig

8

Breeders are always trying to raise better potbellied pigs. They want the best parts of their pigs to get better, and the worst parts to go away. For parents, they will choose pigs that are friendly, look the most like the ideal potbellied pig, and are in good health. Because the size of the parents will decide the size of the babies, it is useful to know how big your pig's parents were. You can not make a potbellied pig smaller by feeding it too little — this would cruelly starve it.

You can tell a lot about how the piglets will grow up by looking at their mother.

Did you know?

Pigs don't see very well. They can smell and hear much better than people. They use these senses to get information about the world. Potbellied pigs have such a good sense of smell that they can be trained as drug-sniffers to help police. Pigs don't sweat very much, so they can quickly get too hot in the sun. Pigs get sunburned easily.

Babies and Piglets

Male potbellied pigs are called boars. After they are **neutered,** males are called barrows. Female potbellied pigs are called gilts if they have never had babies, and sows if they have.

Sows are pregnant for almost four months. They give birth to between one and twelve piglets. They each weigh less than a pound. Piglets spend most of their time drinking milk and playing with one another. As soon as they are born they are starting to learn about the world around them.

Each piglet chooses where it wants to nurse, and will fight off the others to defend its place.

The piglets drink milk from their mother for five to six weeks. Then they are **weaned.** This means they are given solid food to eat and gradually stop drinking milk from their mother. Potbellied piglets are ready to find new homes between six and eight weeks of age.

Pig breeders

Most potbellied pigs are bred and raised by **breeders.** Good breeders follow guidelines on how pigs should be cared for. They keep their pig's housing very clean and take good care of their herd. They choose the parents of each litter carefully to breed the smallest, friendliest, and healthiest pigs possible.

They start to handle piglets soon after they are born so they can get used to people. They usually **register** their piglets.

Good breeders know that potbellied pig pets should be neutered before they are sold. Potbellied pigs that are not neutered do not make good house pets. Most piglets are neutered between six weeks and three months old. They also have **vaccinations,** just like people do.

Because this breeder has started to handle this potbellied pig it will become used to people.

Registries

Registries are organizations specially set up to record information about individual pigs. Many also keep lists of good breeders and vets who know how to treat potbellied pigs. They may hold shows and other pig events. Most give out information about potbellied pigs and answer questions.

This family is choosing its new pet. The breeder will let them spend as much time as they need choosing and will help them find the right one.

11

Is a Potbellied Pig for You?

Most potbellied pig owners love their pets. They talk about how fun and friendly their pigs are. They enjoy how smart and trainable their pets are. But some people choose to get a potbellied pig before they are ready. They can find their pigs too difficult to care for well. Their pets may end up in special pig shelters called **sanctuaries.**

All pets have their good and not-so-good points. Before you decide to get a potbellied pig you should know about them.

Potbellied pigs need special places set up for them to live in.

Yes or no?

Having a potbellied pig means:

- feeding it every day,
- checking its health every day,
- giving it clean water every day,
- giving it a safe home inside and outside your house,
- spending money on food and vet care,
- bathing and **grooming** it regularly,
- playing with it and spending time together every day,
- being **consistent** in training it,
- always treating it with respect and love.

Potbellied pigs are wonderful pets for the right families.

Are you really ready to do all these things, even when you are in a hurry or want to do something else? If the answer is yes, talk with your family about owning a potbellied pig.

Other pets

Potbellied pigs are best as only pets. Small pets in cages or tanks will not bother pigs, but make sure the pig cannot get into the cage! If you already have a cat, it will usually just ignore your new pig. If you have a dog, you could have a problem. Dogs are naturally hunters, and pigs are naturally hunted. Even the best-behaved pet dog sometimes will act as its nature tells it to. You must never leave a dog and a pig alone together.

Some families choose to own more than one pig and really enjoy their larger herd!

How many pigs?

Experts disagree about whether it is best to have one or more potbellied pigs. Most say one pig is best, since it will **bond** with you and your family. Others say pigs are naturally herd animals and feel happiest with other pigs. They also say you will have fewer problems as your pets try to find their places in the **pecking order** of your family, since they will sort it out among themselves and leave the people out of it. Everyone agrees that it does not matter if you have a male or female potbellied pig as long as your pig is **neutered.**

13

Potbellied pig good points

- Potbellied pigs are fun to play with and can be trained to do tricks.
- Potbellied pigs are curious and fun. They like to explore and learn.
- Potbellied pigs show their people affection. They think of them as part of their herd and like to be with them.
- Potbellied pigs do not usually cause allergies.
- Potbellied pigs are quiet pets.
- Potbellied pigs are generally healthy when cared for properly. They like to stay clean and can be housebroken.
- If they are happy and well cared for, potbellied pigs can live a long time. Most live twelve to fifteen years as pets.

Potbellied pigs make good friends.

Walking your potbellied pig keeps it healthy.

Potbellied pig not-so-good points

- Potbellied pigs need a lot of care. They can be more demanding than dogs.
- Potbellied pigs need to play and keep learning or they will get bored. If they get bored, they can find destructive ways to keep busy.
- Potbellied pigs need a fairly large area to live in, with a pool to cool off in when it is hot and a pile of bedding to snuggle under when it is cold.
- Potbellied pigs, like all pigs, need to **root.** If they do not have a place to dig and explore, they will try to root in your carpets, flowerbeds, or garbage cans.
- Potbellied pigs love to eat. They do not know when they have had enough, so you need to feed them carefully. They will learn to beg if you let them. They can get pushy if they see you eating. They can learn to open refrigerators and cupboards to get food.
- Potbellied pigs can easily eat poisonous things . You need to keep poisonous plants and household items away from your pet pig.
- Potbellied pigs are herd animals. Your pig needs to learn its place in its herd, which is your family. Being firm and **consistent** with your pig will teach it that it is not the leader of its herd. A spoiled pig that thinks it is the leader can get **aggressive** and dangerous.
- Potbellied pigs need special vets to care for them. Your pig will need a checkup at least once a year. Treatment for a sick pig can be expensive.
- The **zoning laws** where you live may not allow potbellied pigs.

Anywhere your pig can get into will need to be pig-proofed.

15

Choosing Your Potbellied Pig

Most experts agree that the best way to buy a potbellied piglet is from a good **breeder.** Find a breeder by asking the **registries,** pig clubs, vets, or pet stores. Most breeders know everything about the piglets they sell. They give buyers papers describing what **vaccinations** and vet care the piglets have had. They usually sell **neutered** piglets. Many breeders will have **registered** the piglet with a national **registry.**

You could also adopt a potbellied pig from a **sanctuary.** Many of the pigs at sanctuaries are fully grown and good family pets. These pigs will need to be brought into your home as carefully as a piglet would, but they will already be housebroken and have settled down into their adult personalities. Piglets bought from breeders can be expensive, where as adult pigs from sanctuaries usually cost less.

A good breeder will give you the pig's health and vaccination records and registration papers.

Check that the breeder is well thought of before you buy a piglet there.

16

What to look for

Wherever you go to choose your potbellied pig, you should make sure it is:

- Healthy – bright, active, clean, a good weight – most breeders will guarantee their pigs' health.
- Friendly – it should not try to bite you.
- Handled – a piglet should not squeal too long when picked up.
- **Neutered** – all males and most females should be before you buy them.
- Sound – its body should look right for its breed. It should move smoothly and not limp. It should have bright eyes and not have a runny nose.

This is how a potbellied pig should look. It moves easily and is very healthy.

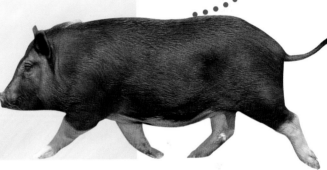

Did you know?

The best breeders and sanctuaries will always be there to answer your questions about potbellied pigs – before you get one and after you take it home. They want you to be sure you know what owning a potbellied pig means before you take the plunge! They will help you find out about **zoning laws** and vets where you live as well.

The ideal potbellied pig

Potbellied pigs are particularly cute. The ideal one is friendly, with a swayback, potbelly, ears that stand up, and a straight tail. The ideal height is less than 14 inches (36 cm), and weight is less than 50 (23kg) pounds. They come in black, white, or black-and-white in patches.

How big?

Because most people get potbellied pigs because they are meant to be smaller than ordinary pigs, they want to know how big their piglet will grow. There are two ways to find out. One is to know how big its parents were, since it will be about the same size as them. Most **breeders** can tell you this. The other is to wait until it is fully grown (about 3 to 4 years of age) and see. Sometimes people may think their pig will be smaller than it turns out to be. They may be unable to cope and may give their pet to a **sanctuary.**

Registering potbellied pigs

Most potbellied pigs are **purebred,** which means they look like other potbellied pigs and have potbellied pig parents. If your pig's whole family tree is known, then it has a **pedigree.** If it is a pedigreed potbellied pig, it can be **registered** with one of the national registries and shown in their shows. If your potbellied pig is not pedigreed, you can still register it as a pet with several of the **registries.** This means its information will be kept, and it can be shown in pet pig shows.

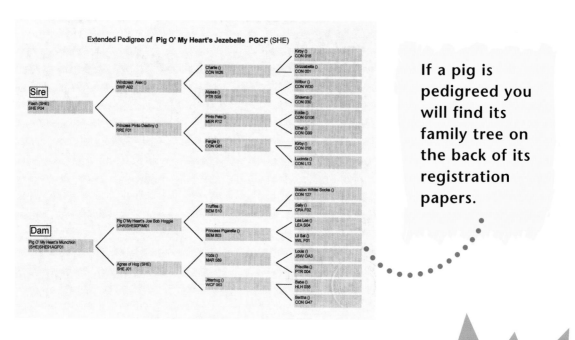

If a pig is pedigreed you will find its family tree on the back of its registration papers.

Permanent ID

It is a good idea to have your potbellied pig permanently identified. A vet can put a **microchip** under its skin. The microchip holds information about your pig. Then, if it is ever lost or needs to be identified, the microchip can be read. Some pigs are tattooed or branded instead.

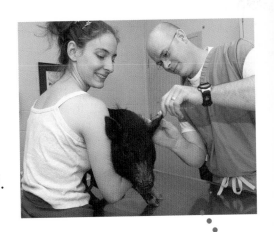

Sponsor a pig

If you are not yet ready to get your own pet potbellied pig, you could sponsor one at a **sanctuary.** This means you can get to know a pig through photos, reports about its health, and stories about its life. You may be able to visit if the sanctuary is near you. When you have spent time learning about "your" pig's life and habits, you might feel ready to have your own.

Having the microchip put in is quick and easy because it is so small. The pig doesn't know it's there after it's in.

Bad habits

Some of the pigs at sanctuaries have been mistreated and have bad habits. As a first time pig owner, you should not try to live with one of them. They will need careful training and a great deal of love and attention to become good pets again.

When not properly trained, some potbellied pigs may develop bad habits.

Your Potbellied Pig's Home

Many potbellied pig owners want their pets to live as part of their families, the way dogs and cats do. While some pigs live only indoors and some only outdoors, most are happiest moving between both each day. However you set up your new pig's home, you must make sure it is ready before you bring your pet home.

This potbellied pig likes its cozy outside house.

Hot and cold

Potbellied pigs are **sensitive** to the weather, so they need special care when it is very hot or cold. Outdoors they need a house with hay to snuggle into when it is cold. A special pig shelter or something like a large doghouse or small stable would make a good house. In the heat, potbellied pigs need shade and water to wade in. The best thing is a child's pool with a few inches of cool water under a shady tree. They don't like drafts, so make sure their outside houses do not face the wind and inside beds are sheltered from open windows or doors. Inside, their beds must be away from radiators and ducts for heat or air conditioning.

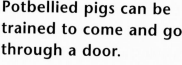

Potbellied pigs can be trained to come and go through a door.

Decisions, decisions

You need to choose between these things before you bring your pet pig home:

- Will your pig go to the toilet indoors or out? Indoors means setting up a litter box. Outdoors means either putting in a dog door or being able to open a door for your pig each time it needs to go. You also need to decide what part in the yard the pig is to use.

- Will your pig be able to run in the whole yard or one part? If you choose one part, you will need to fence that area off. If you choose the whole yard, it will need to be completely fenced in.

- It is best not to give your pigs full run of the house. Choose which rooms it can use and gate them off. Child safety gates that the pig can see through are best. Make sure people go into your pig's rooms often, so it does not get lonely or bored.

Your potbellied pig will be happiest playing with you and feeling like part of the family.

Inside the house

When you have decided where your pig will live inside, you need to give it a bed. The bed should be about twice the size of the pig. Half of an animal crate or a washable dog bed both work well. Put blankets and towels in it to give your pig somewhere to burrow and feel safe and snug. Pigs are like small children — they don't like change. Even though your piglet is small now, it will grow. So choose things that will fit its full-grown size.

If your pig will be litter trained, give it a litter box. The pig should be able to turn easily in it. It will also need an easy way in, so use the bottom of a travel crate or a child's pool with a door cut in. Fill the litter box with wood shavings or newspaper.

Your potbellied pig's bed should be somewhere quiet, because sleeping pigs do not like to be bothered.

You can use a box and newspaper as a litter box.

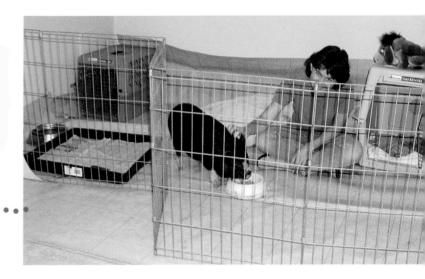

In the yard

In the wild, pigs can move from place to place to get comfortable. In your yard, you need to make sure they will be safe and comfortable in the area they have. First, make sure the fence is strong. Pigs will try to **root** their way out under a flimsy fence. Pigs have few defenses, so make sure your fence will keep other animals and pets out. Second, make sure there is shelter from weather. It can get hot, cold, wet, and windy, so something like a small pig house is a good idea.

Food and water

Wherever it lives, your pig will need a water bowl and a food bowl. Both should be the non-tip kind, since a pig will happily try to root under its bowls and turn them over. The food bowl will need to be bigger than the amount of food, because pigs love to push their food around before eating it.

This potbellied pig's housing is well secured and provides good shelter from the weather.

Pig-proofing

Potbellied pigs will try to get into everything and eat anything. They can be choked or poisoned by many household products and plants. You will need to pig-proof your home before your pig comes into it. This is not something you do only once — pig-proofing means always being on the lookout for new dangers!

It takes time and effort, but pig-proofing keeps your pet safe.

Inside

Pretend your pig is a toddler. First lock all cupboard doors. Then think hard about what might hurt your pig as you crawl around on hands and knees. Move anything sharp, small, or breakable out of reach. Pigs can be hurt by scissors, buttons, plastic bags, light bulbs, and small toys. Cover up electrical outlets and move garbage cans out of the way. Make sure no electric cords are reachable. Things we think of as harmless, such as soap and chocolate, can poison pigs. Look for pig poisons and put them out of reach.

Outside

Because potbellied pigs are very **sensitive** to chemicals, you will need to make sure none has been used on your yard. Poisons that kill weeds, mice, and insects can hurt your pig. Anything used in a motor, such as gas and oil, can also hurt your pig.

Antifreeze, which smells sweet, is very poisonous. Make sure none has leaked from a car or lawnmower. Anything sharp, such as shears or wire twist ties, should be moved away as well. Pigs will try to chew through electric cables, so put cables inside thick plastic pipes and tape up the ends.

Common poisons

In their never-ending hunt for food, potbellied pigs can be poisoned. Some of the pig poisons found in most homes include:

- zinc, such as in pennies and sun block.
- paint, even the kind without lead in it.
- caffeine, such as in coffee, tea, and chocolate.
- cleaning materials, such as cleansers and polishes.
- painkillers, such as aspirin and Tylenol.
- salt, if too much is eaten all at once.
- oleander, even a few leaves.
- algae, the blue-green kind that grows in water in the sun.

This is just a short list. Ask your **breeder** or other experts for more help making a complete list of things to avoid.

Check with your local vet or county agent for a complete list of poisonous plants in your area, then check your yard.

Caring for Your Potbellied Pig

Bringing your pig home

The first time your pig comes into its new home it will be nervous. Be quiet, kind, and gentle. Open the door to its crate and let it come out when it is ready. Move slowly and pet it from the side, never from above. Offer it treats from your hand. Show it its new bed, litter box, bowls, and outdoor space. Walk with it as it explores, and keep talking so it gets to know your voice. Let everyone in the family get to know the pig this way.

To make sure your potbellied pig does not get bored, spend time playing with it and teaching it new tricks.

Potbellied pigs need a routine. They do not like change, so set a schedule from day one that you will be able to follow every day. Give yourselves time for feeding, playing, training, **grooming**, going for a walk, and spending time outdoors.

Behaving well

How you care for a potbellied pig changes as the pig grows up. As a piglet, it needs to learn how to behave. **Behaviors** such as housebreaking and training to walk with a harness and leash are fairly easy to teach with patience. Perhaps more important is teaching your

It takes patience and discipline to train a potbellied pig.

pig how to behave in your family. As an adult, your pig will understand what is expected of it.

How pigs think

It helps to understand how potbellied pigs think in order to decide how you should handle yours. For example, pigs are naturally curious. It will not work if you try to stop yours from exploring or **rooting.** It is better to give it a safe place to root, new toys to explore, and training to learn new tricks.

Everyone in the family must agree on what is allowed and what is not. Some things, such as **aggression,** pushing, or begging for food should never be allowed. Although it may seem unkind to make some parts of your home off limits to your pig, or to never feed it table scraps, it really is best for your pet in the long run.

Leader of the pack

Your pig needs to know who is in charge. The herd leader should always be a person, not itself! Since you are smaller than the adults in your family, you will need to be especially careful to show your pet that you are above it in the herd. Being firm, kind, and **consistent** will help.

If your family works together to learn more about potbellied pigs, you can agree on your rules more easily.

27

Discipline

You need to agree how you will handle **discipline** before your pig comes home. Like people, pigs will test their families to make sure they will stick to the limits and rules they have set. You must always react **consistently** with your pig or it will learn that if it pushes you enough it will get what it wants every time.

Potbellied pigs should never be hurt in order to discipline them. It works better to say "no" and then show the pig a good thing to do. Praise and reward your pig for good behavior. The most important part of good discipline is being consistent and patient. You may need to repeat your "no" and your praise many times before your pig learns something. You must be willing to do this before you take on a potbellied pig as a pet.

Playtime

Potbellied pigs love to play with toys. Babies' toys, empty soda or milk cartons, dogs' pull toys, and rawhide chews are all fun for your pig. It will pull, chew, and **root** around them.

You can make toys for your pet from many kinds of household trash!

This pig loves to travel with its family.

Going for a ride

Hopping in the car is a great way to get your pig out and about. Most potbellied pigs enjoy going for car rides, but some get carsick. You can train your pig to walk up a ramp into your back seat. Most experts agree that pigs should ride inside a travel crate on the back seat, even for short trips. Never leave your pig alone inside your car in hot or cold weather.

If you keep to your routine, it is fun for your pig to add some outings. Well-behaved potbellied pigs are good visitors to places such as schools, nursing homes, and parks.

Taking a bath

Pigs love baths. Because their skin can dry out, they should have baths with shampoo only once a month. Small potbellied pigs can be bathed in a bathtub, but big ones will fit better in a child's pool. Make sure the water is not too cold. If the bath is outside, make sure it is warm so your pig does not get chilled. Follow the bath by rubbing moisturizer into its skin.

What is normal?

Every animal has a different average body temperature. The only way to know what is normal for your potbellied pig is to check its temperature every day for a week. Read it at the same time of day and write it down. The average over the week is your pet's normal temperature. Ask your vet to show you how to take your pig's temperature, or ask an adult to do it.

Using a towel or sponge is a great way to shampoo your pig.

Health check

- Is your potbellied pig eating and drinking normally?
- Is it moving and standing comfortably?
- Is it breathing easily?
- Is it having normal bowel movements?
- If any of these things seem off, check its temperature and call your vet.

Every day

- Clean up your pig's litter box or outdoor toilet area.
- Wash out food and water bowls.
- Check that your pig is in good health.
- Look for **parasites** on your pig.
- Brush your pig's teeth with a washcloth and baking soda.

Potbellied pigs love their food.- If yours isn't eating, it may be sick .

Every month

- Clean ears and check for ear **mites.**
- Check teeth for problems.
- Give a bath with special shampoo.
- Oil your pig's skin with special moisturizer.
- Check your pig's feet and file or trim hooves if needed.

Getting to know your pig's skin will make daily checks for insects and cuts easy.

Feeding Your Potbellied Pig

It will not work to rely on your potbellied pig to tell you when it is hungry. Pigs are always ready to eat! You need to feed your pig carefully to keep it healthy.

How fat is fat?

An overweight pig is a problem. Too much fat puts **stress** on the pig's legs and feet and can even make it blind if fat covers its eyes! Check your pig by pressing your fingers on its back between the spine and the hipbone. If you can feel bones through a good layer of springy muscle, your pig is perfect. Bones too close to the skin or too sunken in a layer of soft fat mean your pig is not the right weight. You need to keep checking your pig's weight to determine how much food is right for it. Talk with your vet or **breeder** about how much food to start with, then keep adjusting until you have got it right. Also, remember that in addition to the right amount of food, a healthy pig needs plenty of exercise.

Here is an overweight potbellied pig. To make s your pig stays healthy do overfeed it.

Potbellied pigs drink a lot of water. They should always have clean water, kept out of direct sunlight. If your pig does not seem to like its water cold, try warming it up a little or adding a very small amount of fruit juice.

How to feed

Potbellied pigs should be fed twice a day. Make sure your pig never eats when and where you eat, because it will learn to beg for your food. Give the mixture of pellets and bran first, in its large non-tip food bowl. Then give it the vegetables and fruit.

What to feed

- Half your pig's food should be pellets of **miniature** pig feed. Ask your vet about the best brand for your pig.
- A quarter of the food can be bran mixed in with the pelleted food. Talk with your breeder or vet about whether your pig should have bran.
- A quarter of your pig's food should be fresh vegetables and fruit. Give mostly leafy vegetables because fruit and starchy vegetables such as potatoes have sugar and **calories** in them. Wash all fruit and vegetables very well before feeding your pig.
- Ask your vet if your pig should have any **vitamins** or **minerals** added to its diet.
- Potbellied pigs also need to graze on grass as much as they want or be fed a limited amount of hay.

33

Training Your Potbellied Pig

Because potbellied pigs are so smart, they are fairly easy to train. The secrets to successful training are being patient, clear, **consistent,** and reasonable. Your pet needs to understand what is being asked, should always have the same signal for a behavior, and only be asked to do things that it can do.

What to train

Some of the **behaviors** you will need to teach your potbellied pig will help you live together happily. After these have been learned, you can move on to fun ones. It is fun to show off tricks and good to keep your training time interesting. You should make regular time for training every day, even as your pig gets older. Pigs can get bored if they are not always learning, and it is best to give them helpful things to learn. Otherwise they could learn to do bad things such as **root** up your carpet or empty your refrigerator!

It's useful to teach your potbellied pig to lie down, since it lets you and your vet easily check your pet over.

Getting started

Plan time when it is quiet so you can both think clearly. Take a minute to get calm, because being kind and patient will help your potbellied pig learn. Always use **positive** rewards such as a treat and praise as soon as it does what you want, not a while after. Never yell at your pig or act angry or frustrated. Pigs will not learn by force. Stop for the day when you or your pet are feeling tired or cannot pay attention any more.

Training sessions

There are books about how to train pigs, and you should get one to help you with the specifics. Generally, a training session takes natural behaviors and turns them into tricks. You use voice and hand commands to tell your pig what to do. When it does the trick, you give it praise and a training treat as a reward. Your training treats should come from your potbellied pig's daily feed, so you do not end up feeding your pet too much. Give training treats flat on the palm of your hand.

After you have mastered the basics, there are lots of other tricks to learn.

Stop it!

Sometimes you will need to stop a pig from doing something. You should say "no" and give it a light tap on its snout. Do not try to hurt its snout, just try to get its attention. Remember how **sensitive** its snout is! Soon just the word "no" will work.

A gentle tap on the snout while saying "no" will train your pig to stop doing something.

Core training

There are many useful things you can teach your potbellied pig. At first, you will need to teach your potbellied pig to be picked up. Then it will need to learn to come when called, wear a harness, and walk on a leash. It will need to be housebroken. Most pigs will have to learn to travel in a crate and perhaps climb stairs and walk up and down ramps. All of these **behaviors** are learned through slow and patient training, starting as soon as you take your potbellied pig home.

Special tricks

Once you and your pet have mastered the basics, you can move on to tricks. Pigs can learn to sit, dance, kneel, jump over and through things, push things along, play piano, and walk over a seesaw.

Housebreaking

It is very important to train your pet to use a litter box or go outside. Either way, you will need to take your pig to the right place, tell it to "go potty" or "go to the toilet," and then wait until it has gone. When your pig goes, give it lots of praise but no treats. Although a piglet can learn fairly quickly, it cannot

Potbellied pigs can learn special tricks!

control its bladder fully until it is six months old. Be ready to clean up accidents and do not let your piglet go anywhere you cannot clean until you are sure it is ready.

Watch out!

Pigs can get very upset if they get scared. They may squeal in a way that sounds like a very loud scream. Pigs that get too upset can really hurt themselves because of the **stress** they feel. If your pig gets too upset, be ready to take away whatever is upsetting it.

Some **miniature** pigs are professional performers, showing off amazing tricks.

Visiting the Vet

Not many **vets** know how to treat potbellied pigs. You need to find one who either already has potbellied pig patients or is happy to learn about them. Try the national **registries** and potbellied pig groups, local **miniature** pig clubs, or **sanctuaries** to find out about good vets in your area. It is a good idea to find your vet before you bring your potbellied pig home. Your vet can check your pig to make sure it is healthy as soon as you get it or even before.

Vaccinations

Most of the dangerous diseases that your pig can get are prevented by **vaccinations.** Your vet will agree what vaccinations your potbellied pig will need to have depending on its age and where you live. You must make sure you take your pet to the vet for its checkups and shots. Some vaccinations only last six months, so you may need to go in twice a year.

Besides checking your pet's health and giving vaccinations, your vet will also try to make friends with your pet.

Going to the vet

Always bring your pet's health records and any papers from the **breeder**. Bring treats, and ask your vet to offer your potbellied pig some of them as a way to make friends. Your pig will take a cue from how you act. Stay cheerful, and your pet will also stay more relaxed.

Keeping calm

Pigs can get very **stressed** if they get scared or hurt. Simple things such as trimming hooves can become life-threatening if your pet starts screaming and acting wild. The best way to keep your potbellied pig stress-free is to train it well. It should be used to being handled, checked over, driven in a car, and taken to strange places. Reward good **behavior** at the vet's with especially nice treats and lots of praise.

Sometimes the vet will need to get to your potbellied pig's stomach, so train it to be held like this.

Remember to stay calm and patient, and not to act worried or upset in front of your pet.

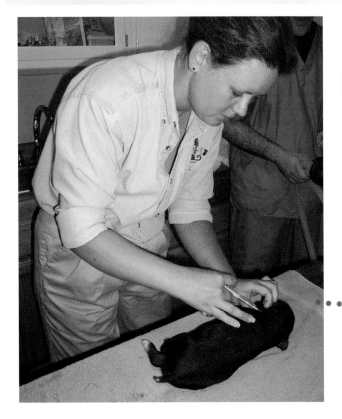

Some Health Problems

Getting sick

Potbellied pigs get different kinds of illnesses.

- **Parasites** — these are usually picked up through the soil while **rooting.** Inside the body they are usually worms. You can treat them by deworming. Outside they are **mites** or **lice.** You can treat them with special washes.
- Digestive problems — diarrhea, vomiting, and not wanting to eat are signs that something is wrong.
- **Respiratory** problems — coughs, colds, flu, and pneumonia can make potbellied pigs very sick.
- Arthritis — sore joints and bones can make potbellied pigs lame.
- Snout diseases — these are problems with the bones or flesh in the snout.
- Cuts and scrapes — keep them clean and watch for infections. If the cut is deep, get your pet a **tetanus** shot.

Pig-to-pig contact

Besides making sure your home is clean and healthy for your pet, keeping your potbellied pig away from other pigs is a good way to help it stay healthy. If you do see other pigs, for example at a show, make sure you keep your pig away from their **feces.** Always bring your pig's own food and water bowls, and don't share them.

At a show, make sure you know what your pig is doing at all times.

Even if they never see another pig, potbellied pigs can get diseases only passed along by other pigs. Germs can be carried into their homes on shoes and clothing. Piglets can get diseases from their mothers. The illness may stay inside them without making them sick long after they are **weaned** and move away. Then something **stressful** might happen that starts the disease.

Getting better

Many diseases are treated with **antibiotics** or other medicines. The vet will tell you the best way to give your pig medicine. Usually pills are hidden in a tasty treat.

First aid

Just like people, potbellied pigs sometimes need first aid. It is a good idea to talk with your vet about CPR, basic first aid, and what medicines to have on hand. If your pig is badly hurt, do what you can to help and call your vet. If it has eaten a poison, call for help right away with as much information as you can about what it ate.

Hiding medicine is the best way to get it into your pig.

Zoonoses

Diseases that are passed between animals and people are called **zoonoses.** Potbellied pigs and people can get things such as **parasites** and flu from one another. They are passed through touching skin, breathing, and eating infected things. The best way to keep you and your pet healthy is to make sure you keep it clean, wash your hands every time you touch it or its things, keep its home and things clean, and make sure its **vaccinations** are up-to-date. Many zoonoses are stopped by vaccinations.

New teeth

Potbellied pigs get new teeth just as people do! At about five months their baby teeth start to fall out, and permanent teeth grow in. They may want to chew a lot while this is going on, just as a teething baby would.

Because some diseases can be passed from people to pigs, stay away from your potbellied pig when you have the flu.

Saying goodbye

Most potbellied pigs live for many years. If you give yours a healthy home, good care, love, attention, and training, it should live a long time. But however well you care for your pet, one day it will die. Sometimes a potbellied pig will just die peacefully at home. This may be a shock to you, but do not blame yourself. There was probably nothing you could have done.

Sometimes you need to be responsible enough to help a pet that is in pain. One day your vet and you may agree that your pet is suffering and there is nothing else you can do to help it get better. It can be very hard for you, but putting a sick potbellied pig to sleep may be the best way to show how much you care for it. The vet will give it a small shot that makes it sleepy. Soon its heart will stop, and it will die. It will not feel pain, just sleep.

As they get older, potbellied pigs sometimes need special care.

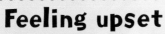

Feeling upset

However it happens, you will feel upset when a pet dies, especially if it has been a friend for years. It is perfectly normal for people — even adults— to cry when a pet dies or when they think of a dead pet.

Keeping a Record

It is great to watch your potbellied pig grow up and become a member of your family. Writing down all the interesting things that happen with your pet is a good idea. Buy a big scrapbook, and fill it with photos and notes. You could start your scrapbook even before you bring your potbellied pig home. Write down what you did to get ready. Put in photos of the day you brought your pet home.

A special diary

It is helpful to note how your pig eats, what it weighs, and what happens at each visit to the vet. If it has any illnesses, write down what happened and how you coped with it. Keep the numbers and contact information of your vet and experts who were helpful in your records. If anything goes wrong again, you can look back at your notes for help.

Potbellied pig shows

There are two kinds of potbellied pig shows — ones for **registered** potbellied pigs and ones for pets. Both are fun to go to. You can spend time **grooming** your pet and practicing the kinds of things you will need to do, such as standing still and walking for the judges. Potbellied pigs are judged on how well

As your pet learns and grows, keep making notes and taking pictures. You will soon have a wonderful record of its life.

CHICO

April 14, 2002
Chico's first day at his new home.

May 15, 2002
Chico learns how to open the refrigerator

September 14, 2002
Chico catches a cold. Mom gives him medicine the vet prescribed.

their bodies match the ideal potbellied pig body. Judges also look for bright, friendly, cooperative pigs. They want to see a potbellied pig walk or trot well, moving easily. After a show, write about it in your scrapbook and paste in programs, ribbons, and souvenirs.

If you decide to show your pet, remember that the idea is to have fun and meet other potbellied pig lovers. It does not matter how well you do, as long as you and your pet have a good time. But maybe your potbellied pig will win ribbons to add to your scrapbook!

Finding out more

There are many other people as interested in potbellied pigs as you are. Maybe they have already started a pig club near you. Find out by asking your vet and **breeder,** or by checking with one of the potbellied pig associations. Pig clubs meet to share information, talk about potbellied pigs, and help each other out. Books, magazines, and good websites are also good ways to find out more. Try your library, pet shop, and bookstore for sources.

Pig clubs and shows are great places to get information and ask questions.

Glossary

aggression behaving in a nasty, pushy, or violent way

antibiotics medicine that fights infection

behavior way of acting, or one specific kind of action, such as lying down when asked to

bond to make a strong tie like family members have

breeder person who raises baby animals to sell

calories amount of energy a food has in it.

consistent always doing the same thing the same way

discipline training that molds the way an animal behaves

feces solid waste matter passed out of the body

grooming cleaning and caring for an animal's body

lice small creature that lives in another animal's hair and sucks its blood

mammal animal with fur or hair on its body that feeds its babies with milk

microchip a very small computer chip that holds a lot of information

mineral substance found in food that helps people and animals stay healthy

miniature something that is much smaller than normal

mite small blood sucking insect

neutered having an operation that stops an animal from having babies

parasite small creature, such as a worm or mite, that lives in or on another creature

pecking order the way a herd is ranked

pedigree an animal that is purebred and has records of its family tree

positive good

purebred an animal that is a clear member of a breed,

registered when an animal's details are recorded by a national organization

registry organizations set up to record information about individual animals, and give out information about the breed of animals

respiratory having to do with breathing

root explore and dig with the snout

sanctuary place where potbellied pigs are looked after.. Most offer potbellied pigs for good families to adopt.

sensitive very easily hurt

stress tension caused by feeling bad in body or mind

tetanus a disease that makes the jaw freeze up

vaccination shots that help protect against diseases

vitamin important substance found in food that helps people and animals to stay healthy

wallow to cover in mud, dust, or water and roll around in it; also the place where a pig does this

warm-blooded an animal that is able to create its own body heat

wean when a baby animal eats solid food instead of drinking milk from its mother

zoning laws local laws that say what is allowed on different plots of land, such as how much land a house must have in order to keep farm animals. Some towns include potbellied and miniature pigs as farm animals.

zoonoses diseases that are passed between animals and people

Further Reading

Kelsey-Wood, Dennis. *Pot-Bellied Pigs: A Complete and Up-to-Date Guide.* Broomall, PA: Chelsea House Publishers, 1997.

Taylor, Micheal. *Pot-Bellied Pigs As Your New Family Pet.* Neptune City, NJ: T F H Publications, Inc., 1993.

Storer, Pat. *Miniature Pigs.* Hauppauge, NY: Barron's Educational Series, Inc., 1992.

Useful Addresses

International Potbellied Pig Registry
P.O. Box 514
Lincoln, CA 95648
(916) 645-9561
www.potbelliedpigregistry.com

North American Potbellied Pig Association
385 Muttart Rd
Neenah, WI 54956
(920) 725-5781
http://www.petpigs.com

American Association for the Prevention of Cruelty to Animals
424 E. 92nd Street
New York, NY 10128
212 876 7700
http://www.aspca.org

Disclaimer
All internet addresses (URLs) given in this book were valid at the time of going to press. However, due to the dynamic nature of the Internet, some addresses may have changed, or sites may have ceased to exist since publication. While the author and publisher regret any inconvenience this may cause readers, no responsibility for any such changes can be accepted by either the author or the publisher.

Index

DUE DATE
